Apocalypse Survival

(Zombie or Otherwise)

By: Leethal

leethalbiker@gmail.com

A How to Manual...

Apocalypse Survival

(Zombie or Otherwise)

ISBN 978-1-304-66137-1

Published by Lee Williams

Apocalypse Survival (Zombie or Otherwise)

Revelation 6:7-8

King James Version (KJV)

"⁷And when he had opened the fourth seal, I heard the voice of the fourth beast say, "Come and see." ⁸And I looked, and behold a pale horse: and his name that sat on him was Death, and Hell followed with him. And power was given unto them over the fourth part of the earth, to kill with sword, and with hunger, and with death, and with the beasts of the earth."

Dedicated to all my fellow "Apocalypse Believers" and Second Amendment Supporters.

God Bless us… and may He have mercy on our souls!

Also dedicated to my wife and daughters… who thinks Zombies are ridiculous!

And my Son John, when push comes to shove, always has my back!

Introduction

I don't care what you believe. Nor should you care what I believe. That being said, it does not matter if you believe in a real Zombie apocalypse, apocalyptic event of ANY kind, Government conspiracy, germ warfare, etc. The point is, regardless of what a person thinks will happen, preparation is the key to survival. This book originally started in 1999 as the "Y2K Survival Manual." It was put on hold because of my belief that the end of the world would NOT occur at midnight on January 1st, 2000. Sometimes it's a bummer being right. I do believe that an apocalyptic event is coming, and maybe soon. Matthew 24:36 "'No one knows about that day or hour, not even the angels in heaven, nor the Son, but only the Father" (NIV). Some Christian faiths believe that prior to the apocalypse they will be "taken up" into Heaven. John 14:1-3 "Do not let your hearts be troubled. Trust in God; trust also in me. In my Father's house are many rooms; if it were not so, I would have told you. I am going there to prepare a place for you. And if I go and prepare a place for you, I will come back and take you to be with me that you also may be where I am" (NIV). Some Christian faiths believe that AFTER the initial apocalypse they will be gathered up into heaven, but only after "proving" themselves. Some believe that only SOME will be gathered. Matthew 24:40-41

"Two men will be in the field; one will be taken and the other left. Two women

will be grinding with a hand mill; one will be taken and the other left" (NIV).

Some people have no religious beliefs and don't think there will be a rapture. Some

people think… you get the idea.

Want to know what I believe? Tough! It doesn't matter, nor should you care

what I think! Why should you give a darn what I think? What do you think? When

do you think an apocalyptic event will happen? Do you really think one will

happen? If so… Are you PREPARED! The overall point is that it is better to be

prepared than dead. It is better to be ready for an event that may not happen, than

sit in the middle of the street crying in the fetal position because you didn't think it

would happen.

Survival is one of the most basic elements that make up every living

organism. Mammals survive; some by hiding or with camouflage, some by

fighting, some by being sneaky, and some by doing whatever it takes to live. What

kind of survivor are you? Obviously you have a desire to survive, or you wouldn't

be reading this! So now you need to assess what kind of survivor you are. Can you

kill an animal for food if necessary? Can you steal to survive in a lawless world?

Can you kill another person in self defense? If you answered "No" to any of these

questions, go curl up in the fetal position in the street and start to cry.

Basic survival can be found in thousands of books at your local Library/Bookstore. If you need have something elaborated on, go read one of those fine pieces of literature first. This book focuses on my opinion, some basics and some advanced street survival, common sense, and some humor specifically in case of an apocalyptic event, such as Zombies. Laugh if you want, new viruses are created all the time. Isn't that right my conspiracy theorists? This book is broken down into survival chapters, some simple and common knowledge (even though common knowledge is NOT common), some more elaborate and explanatory. If the simple ones are "above your head"… go to the Library or Bookstore and read the basics first. I may tell you to have a first-aid kit, but I am not going to tell you how to apply a band-aid. If you can't do the basics, you probably won't survive anyway. Again… fetal position, street, and cry.

The info contained in the following book is by no means a "Bible" to survival; it is simply this author's experience, sarcasm, and opinions talking. You may have a "better way" or a "better idea" than me, if so, awesome! I hope it works for you and you survive the apocalypse. I hope we meet or even team up after the crap hits the fan. I'll be the one wearing the hat…

Apocalypse Survival (Zombie or Otherwise)

Chapters

Chapter One: I Work Out!

I hate to run. But that is no excuse for being out of shape. Exercise is very crucial to survival, hunting, escaping, and survival. No kidding, I said it twice, because it's that important! If you can outrun a bear, you won't get eaten by a bear. If you can outrun a "bad guy" you won't get beaten up by a "bad guy." If you spent your life playing video games in preparation for the apocalypse, kiss your lazy butt goodbye! What kind of training is that? Ever see an Xbox controller on a REAL gun? Ever seen a real gun? Give me a break video kid, you are dead. Get your lazy butt outside now before it's too late to build up your cardio!

Many times when hunting, my hunting partners have asked, how I can keep going, and going, and going... When going for walks, I "walk too fast" or take "too big of strides." I don't think so. I just move along at a comfortable pace, uphill, downhill, dirt, concrete, or whatever. Point is a person needs to be able to walk long distances (or run if needed) once there is no mode of transportation except the feet God gave you! "It's a marathon, not a sprint, unless it's a sprint, then sprint" (Zombieland). Eventually the gas will be gone, the roads will be too congested to travel, and the vehicles will all be broken. Unless you are a mechanic, or one is in your group, you walk OR BIKE! Even if you are a mechanic, unless you're a scientist and can make gas... just sayin'...

So you need some basics to follow to get your cardio up. According to livestrong.com "Basic cardio exercise involves the large muscle groups working in a repetitive motion with little to no added resistance. Legs and arms can be working independently or together to get this effect. This type of training helps strengthen the lungs and heart, and it also helps burn calories. All forms of cardio offer these same benefits."

The steps for basic cardio are as follows. Step one; a five minute warm up. This is simply stretching, getting the muscles in your body to warm up or loosened up. A pulled muscle can become a torn muscle, and unless you're a Doctor, you're screwed. Step two; elevate your heart rate and sweat. That simple, a brisk walk, speed walk, jog, swimming, stairs, or run is all the cardio you need. How long depends on how long it takes you to get that heart rate up and break a good sweat. Step three; depends on your fitness level. Are you built like a pro body builder? Then go pump some iron! Are you a lazy video game playing fat ass? Then just walk fast to start out. Step four; perform your cardio session. Start out with a light two- to three-minute warm-up to get your core body temperature elevated. Increase your intensity to a level that is slightly uncomfortable but not overly intense. Continue at this level for 20 to 30 minutes and finish with a light five-minute cool-down. Step five; remain constant in your regimen. Working out once does not make you physically fit! Start out 2 to 3 times a week and increase to 4 or 5 times a week. Maybe your first workout is 20 minutes, work up to 45 to 60 minutes. Start

slow and get there eventually. You will only hurt yourself going balls to the wall

from day one. Step six; when you are done working out, stretch it out again! The

muscles have been worked relax them by stretching them out and cooling down.

Before, during, and after working out remember WATER (See Chapter Fourteen).

Dehydration is a deadly killer and can cause cramping or worse. No chances; drink

water. Most importantly consult a physician before you take on ANY workout

program or diet (blatant disclaimer).

Eat healthy! Hey soda drinking, and video game playing, chip eating, lazy

butt… How do you feel? Seriously! Do you feel healthy? If you are going to wash

down a milkshake after working out, why bother? It's all well and good to start a

workout program, but diet and exercise together is the key. My wife says,

"Everything in moderation" and "portion control" is the key. My friend Jason who

rides bicycle for hundreds of miles at a time says, "Eat less, move more." They are

both right. Diet does not mean tofu and rice cakes, if a person is trying to lose

weight, he or she must burn more calories than they take in. If a person is trying to

maintain his or her weight, they must burn AS MANY calories as they take in. If

you want to gain weight, take in more calories than you burn. As far as tofu goes,

SCREW THAT! It can't be real food! It has no taste of its own; it takes on the flavor of food it is cooked with! Creepy! Where do you find food after an

apocalyptic event? Chapter Fourteen, so keep reading.

Chapter Two: Double Sure

Also known as the double tap, this little bit of insurance can mean the difference between life and death. Be stingy with your bullets, but not with swinging a bat, make sure. If one hit is good, two must be better! Also remember a gun must be reloaded, you will not reload a bat or sword, and arrows from a bow or crossbow can be recovered. Carry a good machete or a bat with you. Also inconsideration to guns, a 300 winmag is great, but bullets are expensive. For the same price I can get 10 times the amount of 22 bullets. A 22 does the job just as well, 2 to the head kills fine and dandy. More about weapons and bullets later in the book, this chapter is about the double tap.

This chapter wants you "the reader" to know that with every aspect of survival, check and check again. Shoot twice, hit twice, look twice, etc. Do you have _____? Are you sure? Double check. One second to double check can save your life. Be observant! This goes hand in hand with double sure. Practicing this can make it second nature for you. Exercise your mind to be observant. While driving, glance at license plates and then try to remember state and number. Glance at other drivers and then try to quiz yourself about the description. Was it male or female? Did he have a mustache? What color was their hair? What were they wearing? Little details like this can train your mind to observe things and remember them. Eventually it will become second nature and you will learn a life saving technique.

If the apocalypse is non-Zombie related, how well do you know your neighbors? Can you trust them? Can you trust them with your life? How many days do you think it would take for your neighbor to turn to deadly force to supply for his or her family? Those smart guys that study these kinds of things say 4 to 10 days; a little broad for me, so my mentality is ZERO days. I will be ready to take their water, food, clothing, guns, shoes, and more FIRST! Survival, not personal. Unless they are part of "my group", they are NOT part of my group. Part of being double sure means checking your alliances BEFORE the crap hits the fan. This means establish your group of survivors before anything happens. If they think you are nuts, they are not ready and do not need to be a part of your group. More on groups later, back to double sure.

If you have to take your neighbors' car, food, water, guns, or whatever; and you have to do it by force, make sure he or she is not going to get up and take you out. In other words, double tap, shoot twice, and make sure they are down for good! It's nothing personal, just survival, and if you can't handle it, the street is waiting for you to curl up in the fetal position and start crying. I am going to laugh my butt off when the apocalypse happens and there are people actually doing this because they had no better plan. I will take their shoes! Maybe their hat too!

Double sure, two pair of shoes! More on a good pair of shoes later also. Just make

a list and check it twice. You will not regret the extra effort!

Chapter Three: Beware of Enclosed Places

In every horror movie, zombie movie, and slasher flick you have seen the dipstick that goes into a room with only one way in or out. Great plan if you have an automatic weapon and an endless supply of ammo! Otherwise, if you are like everyone else, you are screwed at this point. If I am hell fire bent on survival, and I see you enter a bathroom, storage area, or the like; I am going in after you for your food, water, shoes, and maybe your hat if I like it (doubt it though, my hat is black). If it means the difference between my surviving or not, it sucks to be you, because it's going to be survival of the fittest when the crap hits the fan.

Many a "bad guy" has been trapped like a rat when the SWAT team comes knocking down the door. How did the "bad guy" do? You will probably do just as well. If you have not adopted the mentality of "Me and mine first" then you probably won't be looking for opportunities to follow someone into a one door confined room.

According to mycheme.com "Entry into a confined space can be extremely dangerous. A number of people are killed or seriously injured in them each year." There is no apocalypse yet, and people are ALREADY dying from going into confined spaces? How much worse can it get? "Confined spaces are commonplace in chemical plants and in the process industry generally. This article discusses some of the hazards associated with confined spaces and how these can be managed safely. Please note that every situation is different and that advice is best sought from a safety specialist before attempting confined space entry." I can not believe they have people that study this stuff! "A confined space can be defined as any poorly ventilated enclosed area." (No... Really?!) "Some confined spaces are easy to identify" (yeah... they are enclosed!) "they include storage tanks / vessels, silos, chemical reactors and piping / ductwork. Other confined spaces are less obvious – e.g. trenches, sewers, basements and even rooms with inadequate ventilation. They all either contain or have the potential for containing atmospheres which are hazardous to health. They are usually" (USUALLY!) "unoccupied but occasionally need to be accessed for maintenance or other reasons" (Like Zombies!).

So there you have it, straight from the scientist that studies this stuff! If people are dying from going into enclosed places now, it will be even worse after the apocalypse. My advice... DON'T GO IN THERE! Wouldn't it suck if you went through all the trouble to survive and went into an enclosed area, got locked in and died? Man are you stupid!

The science guy goes on to say (or is this an OSHA guy?), Anyway, "Owing to the hazards present during confined space working, it is important that procedures are in place for when things go wrong" (and they will). "Multiple

fatalities have occurred when rescuers have entered the confined space and have

then been overcome by the same conditions as the original occupants" (that's what

you get for trying to be a hero, see chapter 17). "Therefore, rescue procedures

should be planned in advance" (Brilliant!). "Typically, someone remains on watch

on the outside of the confined space, whilst" (whilst... seriously? This Jack Wagon

is dead when the crap hits the fan. Dude... go curl up in the fetal position in the

middle of the road and start crying now! Whilst...) "work is in progress. They will

be responsible for ensuring that any workers in the confined space are rescued, in

an emergency."

OR... DON'T GO IN THERE! Seriously, what could possibly be in there that

is worth your life? It might even be a trap! A slight bit of paranoia is a good thing

after an apocalyptic event. Be cautious, be alive.

Chapter Four: Safety First

This chapter does not just deal with safety in general. It also deals with bodily safety, mental safety, and firearm safety.

One thing I can say about bodily safety, that sexy little survivor over there, the one making eyes at you, if she will do you for a warm meal or place to sleep, she probably has already, A LOT! Watch out for Nancy McNastysnatch! She might even kill you in your sleep to take EVERYTHING! She is not afraid to use sex as her weapon. Ladies, men are no better; they want one thing. So keep this in mind before you try to repopulate the planet Mr. or Miss perfect genes. You sleep with that person and you just slept with everyone they have. What if they are infected or have some incurable disease. Hey, just run down to the corner store and get some medicine! THERE IS NONE! I already raided the pharmacy and took it all while you were panicking. This is why I talk about groups and the buddy system later in the book. If you don't know someone, be paranoid, you can NOT trust them. Under extreme situations, you may not be able to trust the people in your own group! So what makes you think you can trust a stranger? Make sure, or be dead!

Chapter Five: Groups

(Disclaimer: I am an equal opportunity offender, so if you fit in one of the following descriptions, bummer.) How to create and prepare a group can be the most pivotal decision you will make. It must be small enough to move rapidly, healthy enough to move rapidly, and trustworthy. My essential group would have a Doctor, a Marine Corp sniper, an award winning chef, a mechanic, a couple of construction workers, a gunsmith that can reload ammo, and their families. (People are in better spirits when they have their loved ones with them). The people you should avoid at all costs for your group; politicians (they want to run everything), liars, thieves, lawyers (might as well be politicians), pacifists, PETA people, fat lazy potato chip eating video gamers, stoners, alcoholics, and physically "unfit" people.

If at this point you have asked "Why?" to my ideal group, or who to avoid for a group… Good luck! Maybe your ideal group doesn't have the exact same list, that's cool, but if you don't see the obvious reasons, fetal position, street, cry.

A quality group is going to be made up of people that have talents essential for survival. For instance, Doctor, pretty self-explanatory, but remember this, an emergency room Doctor does well under pressure, keeps his or her cool, and still gets the job done. The rest of my list, I have my reasons, and when you create your group, make sure you have a REASON that the person is in your group. Because their "cool and know how to party" is going to get you killed, common sense people. A celebration is fun, but don't be dumb. Loud parties alert other people, and not the fun party kind of people.

Now the crappy part about your group, be as close as family, but be ready to remove a member. (By force if necessary). Should a member crack, get violent, or jeopardize the group in any way, what must be done, must be done. Nothing personal, just survival.

Chapter Six: Weapons

I love weapons! All kinds of weapons! Guns, bows, swords, axes, knives, bats, you name it, I love it! Any weapon will suit you just fine in the apocalyptic event. It all boils down to personal preference! Do you want to remove threats up close and personal? Try a baseball bat, knife, sword, or axe. They are quiet and don't need to be reloaded. A bow or crossbow are great, quiet and give you a little more playing room. Downside? You have to go retrieve your "ammo" from the target. Guns are great, I really love shooting! The problems are that they are loud, and either you need a lot of backup ammo, or the ability to reload. Also, guns can break down, must be cleaned and maintained. A BAT on the other hand... zero maintenance!

Now, where do I get all of these great weapons? Well, if you are prepared, you already have them! Along with a great supply of ammo and arrows. If not, start picking up stuff now! Craigslist is a great place to find swords, bows, sporting goods, etc. Also check pawn shops, many times a person needs $10 for smokes worse than that set of "chucks" or knife. Most pawn shops have a "cheap bin" of knives that range for $1-$5 all the time.

If you aren't going to stock up ahead of time, you better have a good plan on where to pick up some great items when the crap hits the fan. Looting is illegal now, but in an apocalyptic event, it's not personal, it's survival.

Keep places in mind that have a cache of weapons; pawn shops, sporting goods stores, your crazy neighbor that wasn't able to get home yet, Armory, or a police station. Keep in mind, others may be thinking the exact same, or the armory/police station may be armed AND manned. So plan in advance for your cache of weapons, know how to operate them, and get proficient with them. If you are a bad shot, and I am a good shot (which I am) I win! Thanks for your gun, your boots, and your hat.

One more important note on weapons, the evil enemy of weapons is rust. Make sure you keep your items clean, and maintained. Sharpen, oil, and maintain! A rusty blade can shatter; a sharp blade can slice through a human skull like a hot knife through butter.

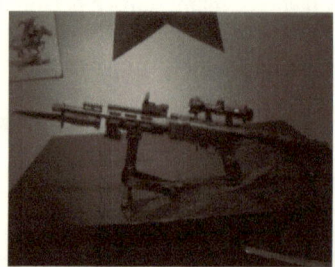

Chapter Seven: Pick It Up, Pack It Light.

Hey look! A recently used campsite! Let's track them and take all their stuff!

Pick it up. Leave no trace that you were there and you make yourself harder to

find, increasing your chances of not getting whacked from behind. When you are

in down time, don't hang a neon sign saying "We're here!" quiet, simple, small,

and compact is the best way to camp. If you're hauling a freshly killed deer with

your party, you are slow, and a target. Take the meat you need, the antlers for

buttons, knife handles, etc. Pack light!

Pack it light means exactly what it says, if you need to move fast, be able to

remove the evidence and move fast. Pack only what you need and leave no sign,

move your butt! If it takes you 30 minutes to pack up and get out, thanks for the

supplies. Packing light means take as little as possible to survive, most everything

else can be picked up, used, and discarded in abandoned homes, towns, etc.

Dehydrated foods are not that tasty, but they are light! Get a flashlight that cranks

for power, or solar. Get a compass and learn how to use it! Carrying batteries is a

pain and unnecessary. Hard candy is a good item to carry, quick little energy

boosts and it doesn't melt like chocolate. Get a space blanket, it's small, light, and

can be used as a shelter or for warmth. A small first aid kit is a good idea, just the

essentials, bandages, ointment, tourniquet, gauze, and maybe a snake bite kit depending on where you are. (Chapter 33) Most cars have a small kit in the glove compartment if you need to acquire one at the last second. Also most businesses have first aid kits in the back room for clumsy employees. Most of the time these First Aid Kits have some great items to take, pain killers, blood stoppers, and other neat essentials. It is important to remember places like that. Most people are thinking the obvious places to acquire these types of supplies, if it's an off-the-wall location; your chances are better of finding what you need.

Obvious places will be hit first, so have a backup plan to acquire essentials if you're a procrastinator. The best plan is to be prepared and have these items in advance. Then be prepared to defend your stuff!

Chapter Eight: My Friend Got Eaten... Now What?

Okay, maybe eaten is an extreme example, let's say for argument purposes killed, shot, run over, or severely sick or injured. I could make this the shortest chapter in the whole book by saying, "Oh well" or "See ya friend" but I won't. The reason I won't is because certain things need to happen when a member of your group gets severely injured, sick, or killed. It goes back to the previous chapter about leaving no trace. Again, fresh dead body, injured group member, or sick friend is a giveaway to your position and existence of the group. As cold as this may sound, bury the dead fast or burn the body away from where you have camped. If they are sick and there is no chance for getting better (or chance of infecting the group) then this person is a hazard to the group. This person must not be allowed to live, if found by others, the ill person may giveaway pertinent information. The same applies if injured, if there is no chance for full recovery or healing, this may slow down the group. As painful as this may be, the individual has become a liability instead of an asset.

In the case of an actual Zombie apocalypse, if the person does get bit, we all know what happens, the person will turn. It's no different a situation than severe illness. Put the person out of their misery, bury or burn the dead, and move out fast leaving no trace. Pulling a sick or injured person along with your group will slow, or hinder all together, the progress of the group being able to move on or defend the group. This will allow others looking for supplies, weapons, and food to take out the group. Would you jeopardize your family or yourself for a group member? I think not. Nothing personal, just survival.

What do I do if the significant other of the injured or sick person wants to stay with their partner until they die naturally? No! Not an option! Now you have lost 2 people from the group, and left 2 people to pass information to a group looking to wipe you out. The significant other will get over it in time, and a live body left behind is a liability. Remove the significant other with other group members and do what has to be done.

Remember, ANY trace is a trail of bread crumbs and can seal your fate. Be wise and do what is best for the entire group. Don't jeopardize the existence of the group for one. Although it seems cold and un-emotional, it has to be done.

Chapter Nine: Hand to Hand Combat Myths (H2H)

There are many incredible instructors that teach hand to hand combat. I am not one of them. I rely on the teachings of professionals in situations like this. Sensei Morey taught me the basics of Shotokan Karate, but I am by no means a "pro".

Even the basics can be very reliable to defend yourself! But if you want incredible skills and discipline, seek out a professional.

First, let's talk about the 10 common myths of H2H combat. I took most of the information from http://www.andrewjackwriting.com/2012/01/25/10-hand-to-hand-combat-myths-that-writers-need-to-stop-using

1. You can't kill someone by shoving their nose back into the brain. It hurts; it breaks cartilage, but won't kill. However, it IS possible to kill someone by striking just ABOVE the bridge of the nose. It requires a tremendous amount of force, so use a bat, not your fist.

2. Getting knocked out is no big deal. BULL! Concussions are cumulative; also it is easier to accidentally kill someone trying to knock them out, than by a controlled method. Brains are fragile!

3. Pressure points work in real fights. Nope. Sorry, but it's not true. There are indeed pain compliance points, but the person you are fighting would have to patiently stand there while you applied them.

4. A kick to the Groin ends a fight. If it lands cleanly and perfectly, it can. But most guys KNOW this is a vulnerable spot and will go to extreme lengths to protect!

5. A kick to the groin is only painful. Reality... a hard kick to the family jewels cans seriously injure a full grown man. However, see above.

6. Grappling beats everything. This is a catch 22, It's not true, but there is an element of truth to it. In UFC competitions a smaller guy named Royce Gracie ran over his larger opponents using grappling art Brazilian Jiu Jitsu. However, his opponents were unarmed. Are you trained in this style of fighting? Thought not.

7. Grappling is useless in real fights. Regardless of what was said above, don't throw grappling out completely

8. You can punch people in the head with impunity. Load of crap. Top of the head, hardest part of the body constructed by one bone. Hand many small fragile bones. Unless your hand has protection, broken!

9. Martial Arts are better. Not really, boxing or Muay Thai are some of the best to learn. I have seen street fighters kick the snot out of martial arts guys. Boxers are unpredictable and hit HARD!

10. Martial Arts guarantee a win. You WISH it was true, it's not. Martial Arts can increase your odds against a non-trained fighter, but it only takes one good hard placed hit to win.

Chapter Ten: Deadly Blows

Now I am going to talk about the basics that I know. Without diagrams I will do my best to give you a good visual. Other information was also taken from http://www.wikihow.com/Be-Good-at-Hand-to-Hand-Combat & http://www.wikihow.com/Disable-an-Adversary-in-Hand-to-Hand-Combat

1. Focus. Know what the opponent is going to do, as soon as he does it or even before. Use distraction techniques! A hand full of sand, dirt, gravel, or whatever to the eyes will either blind them or make them move their guard.

2. Practice. Don't actually go out and get in fights, punching bags are great practice and they won't kick your ass.

3. Don't let size intimidate you. It's true big size, slow moving; the bigger they are, the harder they fall.

4. Aim for the face. If you correctly land a good punch to the nose, eyes water, blood runs, and it at least gives you time.

5. Sneak up from behind. A good blow to the back of the knee with a leg sweep or a fist to the base of the skull can disable an opponent enough to finish the job. Clean fighting? I thought I was fighting to win!

6. If you can get the elbow to the throat, do it! Also grabbing the hair (if they have any) and whipping the head back wards is pretty effective.

7. Take them down. If you can get them to the ground fast and maybe even knock the wind out of them, it's much harder to strike when on the ground.

8. Rhino! Drill your knee to their spine or gut! After you do grab them and drag them down!

9. Neck yank! Get your arms around the neck and yank it up, back, sideways, whatever! Pulling the head up and away from the body can suffocate your opponent.

10. Fast and Hard! If you are gonna hit them, do it FAST & HARD! Go for a KO in 1 blow! If you can't hit hard, practice until you can!

These are very basic, and definitely not ALL the best techniques. Do some research on youtube, or hire an instructor. But remember, there is no fighting "dirty", there is only fighting to win for survival!

Chapter Eleven: A Good Pair of Shoes.

And a backup pair! Boots for me, but you wear what's comfortable for you. I love a good leather pair of combat boots. I also have a pair of boot liners that can be worn inside for extreme cold temperatures. Steel toed boots are great for kicking the crap out of someone, but the toes can get very cold in extreme cold. In addition to a good pair of boots I also have a quality pair of running shoes. When the weather is warm they are cooler on the feet, lighter, and offer great support.

Some boots that I have are camo pair that is for extreme cold, black leather with quick zip sides, a pair of tan desert military issue, and a pair of steel toed biker boots. My running shoes are quality leather that has webbing to allow the feet to breathe and stay dry; they have very good support and are comfortable to wear for many hours at a time.

In addition to a good pair of boots or shoes, keep your feet dry! If you step in water and the boots/shoes get wet, change shoes and don't wear them until they are dry! If you have wet feet in leather boots for hours at a time, it can cause some serious problems. If you wind up with feet issues and can't walk, you are prey.

Chapter Twelve: Survival Pack

The following was taken direct from http://www.isu.edu/outdoor/survkit.htm there are some things I don't agree with which I will go into.

The Do-it-yourself Coffee Can Survival Kit

This is a compact kit that can be carried in the car, on the boat, or in a pack for hunting, hiking, exploring, etc. Most of the contents will fit in a one-pound coffee can which doubles as a pot for melting snow and device with which to dig an emergency snow shelter. (However, if you can carry it, include a small shovel. It is far, far better than trying to use a coffee can.) You should be aware that if this kit is carried while on hiking or hunting trips, you still need to carry the other Ten Essentials not included below.

Keep three points in mind when putting together a survival kit. First, make it small enough that you'll actually carry it and not leave it home. Second, use the list as a guide and customize it to your needs. For instance, if you are allergic to insect bites, bring the appropriate medicine, or carry appropriate wrap if you have knee problems.

Thirdly, bring enough to enable you to spend at least one night out. It is usually the first 6 hours that determine whether you'll be able to survive an emergency. If you can make it through the first night, then your chances are good that you can make it a few more nights if necessary.

Thanks to Allan Priddy who helps teach the Wilderness Survival class for putting this list together.

General Items

Braided nylon rope (25 feet), Mirror, Matches (2 boxes), Fire Starter, Poncho (bright orange to attract attention), Toilet paper, Candle (wrapped in aluminum foil), Paper and pencil, Fishing line, hooks, split shot leads, Knife, Whistle, Money (2 nickels, 2 dimes, 2 quarters, $20 bill: helpful for making phone call or paying for gas if broken down along highway), Garbage Bags (2 large size bags), Bright orange surveyor's tape.

Author's note: Nylon rope – can be replaced with paracord, and braiding it into a bracelet, necklace, lanyard, etc. makes it wearable and takes up less space in the pack. Poncho – in this situation do NOT have a bright colored poncho. Money – pretty much useless dead weight after an apocalyptic event. Another great fire starter is to take the cardboard egg containers, pack dryer lint in them, melt wax over the top. You can cut them apart individually at this point if you prefer.

Repair Kit

Sewing kit, Dental floss (It's strong and useful as thread for sewing, or a fishing line or for lashing branches for improvised shelters.), Safety pins, Wire (bailing wire).

First Aid Kit

Moleskin, Sterile pads (2 x 2 and 4 x 4), Sterile Gauze, Neosporin, Bandaids, Aspirin, First Aid Tape.

Author's note: This list can be expanded; tweezers, surgical scissors, curved needle for stitching, forceps, arm sling, medications, etc.

Nourishment

Honey Packages (available in small foil packages available at convenience stores), Instant Soup or tea (a couple packages).

Author's note: These are great suggestions and I like that the convenience store reference is listed. After an apocalyptic event many things will be cleaned out of stores, but little packets like that will be more so available. Also dehydrated foods and a filter straw or filter bottle.

Optional

> Folding saw, Compass (learn how to use), Hard Candy.

> Author's note: Folding saw can also double as a weapon, good call!

Carrying container

> Coffee Can (1 lb size) or nylon stuff bag

All contents except the plastic bags and the optional items will fit in a 1 lb coffee can. (Or you can flat "Spam" cans or oval-shaped containers available at outdoor stores.) The plastic bags can be affixed to the outside of the can with a rubber band. To keep things from rattling in the can, wad up some wax paper and stuff it around the items. The wax paper stays dry and also doubles as a fire starter. To save weight the contents can be placed in a stuff bag and a metal cup can be used instead of the coffee can.

> Author's note: Metal coffee can is heavier than the plastic ones, so save the weight! Use the plastic coffee can and if you can substitute any other items above with something lighter or smaller, do it! The plastic one is NOT suitable for boiling water though.

Author's note: Although this was mainly about the "survival can", I would like to add that in a survival pack, take a change of clothes! Clean clothes, clean underwear, and clean dry socks. Store them in a Ziplock bag to keep them dry. Children should also have a backpack with some items; this will provide training now for when they get older. The child's pack can have items like a comfort toy or stuffed animal, coloring book and crayons, healthy snack bars and/or candy, bottle of water, and clean underwear and socks. As mentioned, this not only prepares the child for learning a skill needed for life, but gives them some comfort for down time. A loud unhappy child can be a dead giveaway.

I love my back pack…

Chapter Thirteen: Relaxation

Scotch, and maybe a cigar, a couple of the things that will make me happy after an apocalyptic event! There are a lot more items on the list, like twinkies, a good steak, dark micro-brew, good music, a comfortable bed, cognac, and you get the idea. The best part of surviving an apocalyptic event is being able to remember and do the things that brought us pleasure before it happened. While some things may not be able to happen at all the more time goes by, enjoy what you can. Also find new things to enjoy that will be a part of the new world. We have no idea what those are yet, but as the new world develops, we will.

Liquor stores will be hit pretty quickly, so if a good bottle of 12 year old single malt Scotch is going to be your relaxation, get it now and hold on to it. If you didn't stock up, know who your friends are that drink it! Don't be picky! If you are a "specific brand" of Scotch, you may have to settle for a different brand. All of this applies to anything on your list, even if relaxing is cuddling with your Teddy Bear, you may have to find yourself a new Teddy bear. But most importantly, if you are going to relax with a drink or a smoke, be aware. Too much can make you vulnerable, a smoke signal can give away position, so be smart when you relax, remember you may have to haul butt fast! So keep your wits about you.

So stock up on a few comfort items to take with you or have in your fortress, but if you are moving, don't take too much in weight. A flask is lighter than a large bottle, a couple of small cigars are easier to lug around than a humidor, and a backpack guitar is smaller and lighter than a full size one. Be smart and practical, while creature comforts are nice, they are NOT necessary. Survival is the key, not relaxation.

So relax, it's okay, but do it intelligently, don't jeopardize yourself or your group for a couple of minutes of down time.

Chapter Fourteen: Clothing, Shelter, Food, and Water

The four basic things needed to survive for any mammal, human or otherwise, are Shelter, clothing, food and water. Take any one of those items away and you are decreasing your chances of survival dramatically, or completely!

1. Clothing: A human being can die from exposure because of hypothermia in cold water in a matter of minutes. Remember this; Hypothermia, that's the way to go. You freeze real fast and you die real slow. Cute little poem, but true! How painful does dying this way sound? Also important to remember is "Cotton Kills!" Wool clothing is the best defense against hypothermia. Cotton dries from the outside in (towards the skin) keeping the skin cold and wet longer. Wool dries from the inside out, wicking moisture away from the skin, increasing your chances of survival. Warmth is your best adversary, and also being dry. If you fall in a freezing river, get fire and dry clothes immediately! Have an extra pair of clean clothes with you. Personal hygiene is still important, clothes to wear while washing the other set, clean socks, underwear, etc.

2. Shelter: Again, dying from exposure is no fun and can happen very fast. Remember the space blanket? How about the paracord? You have the

makings of a shelter! A shelter needs to be no more than a wind break to keep out the cold and/or wet. A lean to can be made rather quickly and easily also, or find a covering such as a cave. (But make sure it's not occupied! Also this is an enclosed space, remember this from earlier?)

3. Food: Although many factors can come into play as to how long a person can survive without food, as a general rule, go with 8 weeks. Unbelievable isn't it? According to the website http://adventure.howstuffworks.com/survival/wilderness/live-without-food-and-water1.htm there are many factors that fall into play here.

a. Being strong and in good physical shape can help you survive longer, but so does having extra body fat. The body stores energy needed to live in the form of fat, carbohydrates and proteins. The carbs are the first thing to be used up without more food coming in. The fat goes next, which explains why people with more of it can survive longer. Then the proteins go. If you get to the point that your body is using up proteins, basically the body itself, then you're in bad shape.

b. Your metabolism also plays a role. Metabolism is what converts food into energy. If you have a slow metabolism, you'll burn your food intake slower and be able to go longer without replacing the food energy. If you go without food, your metabolism will adjust accordingly and slow down on its own -- basically doing what it can to pitch in for survival's sake.

c. Climate is a major factor too. The bad news is that both cold and hot weather are no good if you have no food. The good news is that extreme heat and cold will kill you in other ways before you have a chance at starvation. But in terms of living without food, heat means faster dehydration -- cold means more energy is burned to keep the body's temperature at a cozy 98.6 degrees Fahrenheit (37 degrees Celsius). If you're lucky enough to be in mild temperatures, you'll be able to live a little longer without food.

d. Some symptoms you may see if you go more than a couple of days without food are: Weakness, Confusion, Chronic diarrhea, Irritability, Bad decision making, Decreased sex drive, and Immune deficiency.

e. Advanced starvation will cause your organs to shut down one by one. People in the throes of severe starvation might experience the following: Hallucinations, Convulsions, Muscle spasms, and irregular heartbeat.

4. Water: A lot less forgiving, a body without water. In extreme hot conditions without water, dehydration can set in within an hour. Humans need water to live, plain and simple. We lose water through sweat, urine, feces and even breathing. This water needs to be replaced in order for

our organs to continue to work properly. In severe heat, an adult can lose

as much as 1.5 liters of water through sweat alone. The main risk

without water in high heat is that your body temperature will continue to

rise and you'll suffer from heat stroke. Drinking water will cool you

down and lower your core temperature.

a. With mild dehydration, you'll experience the following: Lack of
   saliva, Decreased frequency of urine, Decreased output of urine, Deep
   color and strong odor in urine,

b. Moderate dehydration: Even less urine, Dry mouth, Dry and sunken
   eyes, Rapid heartbeat

c. Severe dehydration: No urine, Lethargy and irritability, Vomiting and
   diarrhea

d. The final stage of dehydration is shock. This is characterized by blue-
   gray skin that's cold to the touch. A severe drop in blood pressure
   produces this coolness.

e. Now back to the question at hand. How long can you go without
   water? Assuming you're in reasonable shape and in ideal conditions --
   that is, not in the heat or cold and not exerting, a human can probably
   live for about 3 to 5 days without any water. Healthier humans can
   live another day or so longer. This isn't something you should test.

While people may fast or try a body cleanse without food, you should

absolutely never go without water for more than a day. The Mayo

Clinic recommends drinking about eight cups of water a day, although

there's some debate about this number. Some physicians say less is

fine, while others say the number should be closer to 10 cups or even

more.

Regardless of the debate, Hydration is important, Eat when you can, Shelter

yourself, and have good quality clothing. Cotton Kills!

Chapter Fifteen: Everyday Objects as Weapons

Many everyday items can make a good defense weapon. Here are some examples, and by no means is this an entire list, just some of the obvious ones I came up with.

1. A wooden handle from a broom, shovel, pool cue, etc. Sharpen the end and you have a spear. You can also fasten a knife on the end to work as a spear. Also makes a great Bo staff.

2. A tire iron, not the 4 way type, but the single lug tire iron. This makes a great compact club and is very effective for skull smashing and bone breaking.

3. An ink pen, it can be used to jam into the eye or throat area.

4. Rocks, a good size baseball shaped rock is a great projectile for smashing and throwing.

5. Scrap metal, can be sharpened and used as a shank.

6. Keys, clutch them in your hand with a key or two protruding between each finger. Great for slashing at the face of an attacker or punching soft tissue.

7. Sand, gravel, rubbing alcohol, alcohol, cologne, perfume, bleach, or sand; can be used to throw in the face of an opponent. Not necessarily a weapon, but blinds the threat temporarily or makes the opponent shield themselves,

leaving vulnerable targets open. Any household cleaner or household

chemical can also be used to blind and adversary.

8. Rope, electrical cords, belts, and hoses can be used as a strangling weapon.

These are readily available just about everywhere.

9. Broken glass, scissors, garden rake, razor blades, and other fun toys. Used

properly work just as good as a knife. Use your imagination and use

whatever you can grab fast!

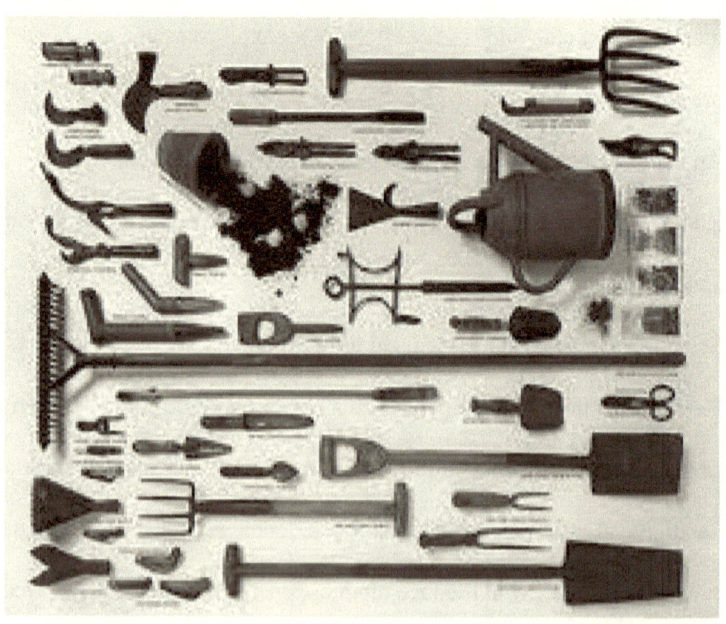

Chapter Sixteen: Find a Penny, Pick It Up…

Money will be worthless in an apocalypse type event. However… certain items that you can pick up can be used for bartering! Just remember, pack light, and don't be hauling around an entire case of Scotch, looking for me, to trade for my extra pair of boots. Also be careful WHO you barter with! "Hey, thanks for trading!" BANG! Now you dead and I have an entire case of Scotch and kept my extra boots Sucker!

Bartering is becoming more popular daily, and will be used even more after an apocalyptic event. When you see a knife, pick it up, bullets that don't fit your guns are a great bartering item. Candy and other excess food items that you may access to will be great for bartering (I found a candy truck and I hid it!) Medication will be a powerful bartering tool, pain killers, tums, bandages, sinus meds, antiseptics, etc.

There a lot of great little bartering items, but you really need to be careful who you barter with and HOW you barter. Always have backup, someone from your group being an observer with a shotgun is a good idea. Never bring more than you intend to trade with you. If go to barter one bottle but are carrying three, you could be losing all of them, either from the barter or being robbed. If it seems too good to be true, it probably is. Be leery of "really good" deals, they may be a setup for disaster. Most importantly, trust your gut. If it doesn't sit well, seems

suspicious, or just doesn't feel right, don't do it, run, it could be a trap. Better to

run away and live to trade another day.

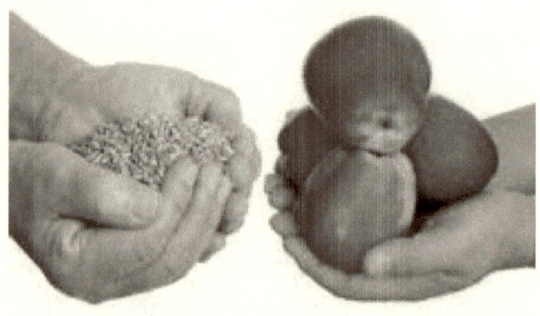

Chapter Seventeen: Don't Be a Hot Shot, or… Humble Thyself

Keeping a low profile can be essential to survival. This isn't the movies; a

Hero always saves the day and lives in the movies. This is real survival and trying

to be the Hero can get you killed. See that damsel in distress? First you have to ask

yourself who tied her up, and then ask why. Probably she works with a group that

lures Suckers in to be killed and robbed. Be leery of every situation that makes you

think you are going to be a Hero. "But if I save the damsel in distress, she will be

forever grateful!" Yeah… let me know how that works out for you Dudley

Doright. Even if she really DOES need rescued and you succeed; you just made an

enemy of the person or persons that had her tied up. Playing Hero can get you

killed, think about the surroundings and situation before you die.

Humility is a great attribute. Want to know why? Because, after an

apocalyptic event, you are no better than anyone else. Seriously! You were a very

successful Stock Broker before all this crap went down?! Wow! That is SO handy

now! NOT! Can you shoot? That's a skill! Understand? You are in the same

situation as every other survivor on the planet. It doesn't matter what you did

before the apocalypse, it's what you can do now that matters. So bring your pride

down a couple of notches and be a useful member of the new society. 2 Chronicles

7:14 says, "and My people who are called by My name humble themselves and pray, and seek My face and turn from their wicked ways, then I will hear from

heaven, will forgive their sin, and will heal their land." My guess is, as many times

humility is mentioned in the Bible, it must be important.

One other important thing to consider about being a Hot Shot, most people

think they are arrogant pricks. People hate swelled heads and despise can lead to

you being ousted from a group, or worse, getting your butt kicked or killed.

Chapter Eighteen: Preparation Mentally

By knowing an event may happen and preparing for it, can make you mentally able to handle it when it does hit the fan. It's no different than psyching yourself up for the big game. You are mentally prepared for the game and you can go out and kick butt! There is a TON of information about preparing mentally as an athlete... Peachy... I'm not playing Tennis here! That being said, we need COMBAT mental preparedness. Who better to provide this than the military? More specifically the Navy Seals! Here is an article straight form the "SEAL Survival Guide: A Navy SEAL's Secrets to Surviving Any Disaster" written by Former Navy SEAL and American Survivalist Cade Courtley.

The brain is the strongest muscle in the body. You've heard stories of how combat soldiers have been shot repeatedly but were not aware of it until the fight was over. These stories are true, and the power to do such things comes from the mind and can be tapped into by practicing mental preparation. This practice can allow you to far exceed your physical limitations. Just as you train other muscles, you can train the brain with mental-preparedness exercises -- and you don't need to go to the gym to do it! It's an exercise you can do anywhere. I can't stress enough how important mental preparedness is for surviving and enduring any life-threatening situation that you could encounter. This is how you practice it.

Emergency Conditioning (EC): Make the Unknown Familiar

Using visualization techniques is a good way to practice what we call

emergency conditioning (EC). I will highlight this phrase throughout the guide and

explain the types of visualizations that are most effective in survival scenarios. It

means conditioning the mind in advance of emergencies, thus producing

psychological strength in times of crisis. This is also referred to as "battle-

proofing" or "battle inoculation" by military personnel. Example: A soldier laying

on his cot imagines a nasty firefight with the enemy; including what it will sound

like and smell like, the heavy breathing, and the utter exhaustion.

If the brain imagines something in deep and vivid detail, it will become part

of a person's "experience files." This visualization exercise will actually fool the

brain into believing that you have already experienced this event. You can tap into

these files at will by hitting the play button that starts the "movie" of what you

have already visualized and planned. It will seem more or less familiar if ever you

are confronted with a similar experience. This internal battle-proofing gives you an

incredible advantage.

Create a Trigger

One of the last things you need to do as part of creating mental preparedness is develop what I call your trigger. In order to do this, you must dig deep and identify the single most important thing in the world to you and make a mental portrait, so to speak, of this image. This is what you will use to ignite many of the essential qualities needed to survive. This trigger is the thing that makes you want to live, no matter what comes your way. The most effective trigger will be different for everyone. For some, the trigger will be the image of their child, whom they want to be there for and whom they want to see grow into a man or woman. For others, the trigger image could be elderly parents who need them.

Your trigger image can change as priorities in your life change. When I was going through BUD/S, my trigger was seeing myself walking across the stage at graduation and looking out at family and friends as I was handed my certificate of completion -- that image made me endure. But once I got to a SEAL team and took on the incredible responsibility of leading men into life-threatening situations, my trigger was the image of all my men returning from a mission unharmed. I was not going to attend any of my guys' funerals -- not on my watch -- and that made me pull my trigger and do whatever needed to be done to keep my men alive.

Your trigger could be an aspirational one -- i.e., thinking that nothing is going to rob you of your life before you achieve your goal. It's as powerful as a protective trigger, such as saving the life of a loved one or protecting a member of your team. Both work, as long as you take the time to make this an extremely vivid visualization. Let it burn into the files of your mind. You must be able to say, "I will live and endure anything for this."

This image or visualized goal is now your trigger. You will use this most important memory file as the ultimate motivation to get you through anything life throws at you. But to maintain the effectiveness of your trigger, you should save it for only the direst situations. Life or death . . . Pull that trigger!

Situational Awareness

In military-speak, situational awareness is defined as the ability to identify, process, and comprehend the critical elements of information about what is happening to the team with regard to a mission. More simply, it's being aware of what is going on around you.

Because I know the importance of situational awareness during battle, I must admit I get annoyed by the vast number of people who go about their lives without paying even the faintest attention to where they are or what's happening around them. It puts them and the general security of society at risk. These are the very people who most often get victimized or end up on the casualty list. The next time you go to a crowded shopping mall or airport, you will be amazed to observe how many people seem to be oblivious to their environment, insulated in their own world. As we will see, airports and malls, in particular, are two places where you should be absolutely vigilant and aware of your surroundings.

Of course, there are environments that require different levels of situational awareness. If you're at home or at a resort, you should fully enjoy the peace and relative security these places afford. As you will learn, these places can be made safe and allow us to relax and enjoy life. On the other hand, airports, the streets of a foreign country, or a crowded stadium event, for example, are not the environments in which to take a mental vacation. You owe it to yourself to stay alert. Just like visualization, situational awareness drills can be practiced anywhere. Make it a game you play using the following checklist:

Situational Awareness Checklist

- Try to guess what individuals around you are thinking or doing.
- Look for odd behavior or things that seem out of place.
- Determine where you'd go if you had to seek immediate cover from an explosion or gunshots.

- Find the two closest exits.

- Determine whether someone is following you or taking an unusual interest in you.

Imagine this scenario: You see a guy at a shopping mall wearing a heavy coat, holding a cigarette with two inches of ash on the end of it, and he's not inhaling. He continues to look over his right shoulder at another guy fifty feet away with a similar heavy coat. It is 90 degrees outside. If you practice even the slightest measure of situational awareness, this scene should set off alarms in your head. In terms of honing your situational awareness, you may find it helpful to think of yourself as trying to note variances against the baseline, or what is normal.

Author's note: I never sit in a public place with my back to the door. Thank You Former Navy SEAL and American Survivalist Cade Courtley for this information. This book is one of the best I have ever read on the subject and I highly recommend getting a copy and reading it if you are serious about surviving. Pretty sure Cade Courtley will be a survivor and I hope when we meet after the apocalypse, we can be friends. I sure as Heck don't want this guy on my bad side! Also Cade, thanks for your Service to our country! GO NAVY! (I am also former Navy, Submarines, MT3)

Buy this book! Thanks again Cade for your service!

Chapter Nineteen: Peace in the Valley (or Group)

Be a peacemaker, not a drama queen! I have two daughters in public school and I could write an entire book on the drama my girls have to deal with on a daily basis. "So and So said this about So and So's best friend and her boyfriend is mad at So at So's cousin for saying it too and So and So aren't talking anymore and because So and So is upset they don't want to be friends with So and So anymore and now they won't answer my texts!" I can only imagine what my face must look like when this happens at home. I'm pretty sure I look like I just had a frontal lobotomy... duh... okay...

Drama creates stupidity. It's not helpful. Being a "backstabber", gossip goddess, drama queen, or rumor spreader is dangerous, it will only come back to bite you in the butt. Trying to cause discontent in the group may get you what you want for a short period of time, but in the long run you will make a lot of enemies. Do yourself a favor, if it's not helpful, shut up!

The difference between a leader and a loser? A leader creates an example others want to follow. A loser creates a situation that no one wants to be a part of. If you are not going to be the leader of a group, be a team player. Do what is good for the group and benefits the group. Your survival may depend on the group someday, don't let the past come back to haunt you. Everyone knows that "What goes around comes around." So again, do yourself a favor, Shut up, don't cause

drama, and most certainly do NOT be a So and So!

Chapter Twenty: Saving Your Energy Until Needed

In chapter one it says, "It's a marathon, not a sprint, unless it's a sprint, then sprint" (Zombieland). If your group is a moving group, then move at a steady pace, don't push it. Try running a mile and then boxing. If your group is moving all out and suddenly finds themselves in a survival situation, it's probably not gonna work out best to your advantage to say, "wait... let me catch my breath... then we can defend ourselves... I am too exhausted to fight..." Don't bother, you're dead!

You all have heard "slow and steady wins the race". It's true in this situation, walking at a decent pace from place to place will save your energy until you need it for a survival situation. Watch a marathon runner (see above) they start at a nice steady pace and continue the pace until it's time to win, and then BANG! Like a bullet out of a gun, they end the race and win.

Now, this doesn't mean sit around like a slob until you need to use your energy. Dumb. Go back and read Chapter One. Even if you are a stationary group or individual holding up, you still need to be prepared to defend, survive, or move. Sitting in a corner sucking your thumb because you're afraid and in a "safe" location isn't helping you at all. Go to the middle of the street, curl up in the fetal position, suck your thumb, prepare to be a victim; you might as well make a cardboard sign to lie next to that says, "Waste of Life, Victim, and Kill Me Now."

Chapter Twenty One: Useless Places

After an apocalyptic event is ANY shelter useless? Not really. But... there are places that will be less useful or more dangerous because of the apocalypse. Remember in Chapter 3 discussing enclosed places? How about Chapter 14 talking about shelter? If you take those two chapters and combine them you get the majority of Chapter 21.

What places will be useless after an apocalyptic event? For shelter, quite a few will be useless. Take for instance the majority of office buildings; once they are looted for anything that can be helpful, not a great place to be. The glass is not bullet proof; most of them have a LOT of glass and have no privacy or security. It's the equivalent of being the fish in the fish bowl with the cat sitting there licking its lips.

Enclosed places (refer to Chapter Three) are useless places. You are cornered and have no way out of an emergency situation. If there is one exit, and you are blocked from that exit, you are now a victim. Stay away from useless places that don't have more than one way out. The same goes for elevated locations; if you are in a high rise with one door to the hallway to access the stairwell... sitting duck.

Chapter Fourteen talks about shelter and anyplace that is SAFE and provides shelter is NOT useless. Safety first people! Secure is better if you are a stationary group. Have your group take over a bank, hospital, armory, prison, or any place with bullet proof glass or no glass. A secure place that is made of steel or brick will better your chance of survival. It would however be a good idea to wait until after the place is looted. Seriously, if the drugs are gone from the hospital, you don't have as many visitors and it's easier to defend from a few than a hoard! Bank, who wants money? Use it for warmth and burn it; makes a great fire starter, or toilet paper. After all the weapons are taken from the armory, it's useless except for shelter, and what a secure building! A prison was made to be secure and keep people in, so why can't it keep people out?

So a useless building can be useful after an apocalyptic event, and a useful building in the past can now be useless. So choose wisely, make sure it's secure, attack proof, escapable, and solid.

If you are a wandering group and look for shelter from place to place, make sure it's not already occupied before you decide its home sweet home. Otherwise you may be walking into a fight with someone defending what's already theirs. The last thing you want is a battle that can waste or lose resources. Be safe and be SMART when it comes to shelter.

Chapter Twenty Two: Escape Plan

Didn't I just talk about this in the last chapter? Oh and in Chapter Three? Yes! It's so dang important that it needs to be readdressed! If you have no way out, you are a rat in a trap! Also in Chapter Eighteen about mental preparedness, Cade spoke of planning an escape route when you enter a building, and I spoke of not sitting with my back to a door. These are ALL part of an escape plan. If you have a group and there is a place that needs to be entered to get supplies, play it smart. Two enter armed to cover each other and the rest of the group posts outside armed to protect the people entering. Simple plan, but effective.

The most important thing you can do when entering a location (or even before) is to plan how to get out. When I go to the mall with my wife, I am armed (concealed of course) and know where every exit is; even the back doors in each business. Why do I take the time to know every door? So I can live! If some Jack Wagon comes in with a plan to shoot the place up, he/she better know the building better than me, he/she better spot me quick, and he/she better take me out before I get a shot off. Survival Baby!

Anytime you enter a building, start planning your escape! Not just as practice for after an apocalyptic event, but for survival today! There are a lot of crazy people in the world and we hear about them in the news every day; mall shootings, school shootings, church shootings, etc. Be a survivor today or you won't be around to try and be a survivor after the apocalypse. Know the building, know the exits, know your surroundings, find items that can be used as weapons, recognize suspicious people, and be aware of areas that are unsafe.

Be prepared and be a survivor!

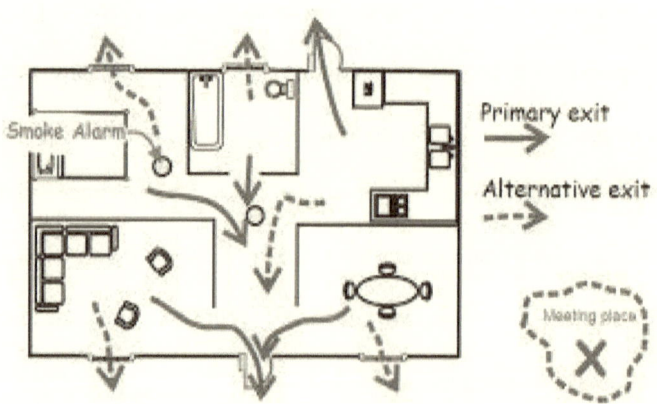

Chapter Twenty Three: Essentials That Don't Fit in Backpacks

Everyone has those "special" items that just won't fit in a pack. Mine would include more nonessentials than essentials honestly; but we are here to discuss ESSENTIAL items that won't fit in a pack. Again, my opinion, you may have other items you consider essential that I don't mention, and I may list items YOU don't consider essential. Good for you, but this is my book, not yours!

Here are some items that may or may not be essentials that won't fit in a standard backpack: Sleeping bag, axe, shovel, water storage container, tent, emergency radio, your extra boots, a tarp, rifle, extra ammo, portable camp stove, gas lantern, fishing pole, a generator, and a bicycle.

While this list is by no means exclusive, it does have some valid points. By no means is a generator an essential item. Nice to have? Yes! But not essential. The same could be said about the portable camp stove if you are fire cooking, but remember that a camp stove doesn't create smoke like a fire. A bicycle may not seem essential, but in a jammed up traffic area it may be the only means (other than walking) to get through. A bicycle is faster than walking, light, and requires no gas. I suggest getting one, a mountain bike with good all terrain tires, not a beach cruiser or racing bike. A good bike can get you almost anywhere.

Chapter Twenty Four: Using Your Brain for More than Kibble

The problem with common sense is that it is NOT common. I am amazed every minute by lack of good judgment made by the human race, and oddly enough these are the people that seem to breed the most. I have some friends that are really nice people, but honestly, they could get lost in a closet. Not the kind of person I would want in my group.

In Chapter Eighteen, Mental Preparedness, it talks about the brain being the most powerful muscle in the body. Not the "strongest", but the most powerful. Why? Take it out of your body and function. Powerful because it controls everything you are! That being said, I know a lot of people that seem like the brain HAS been removed. "If I only had a brain." (Scarecrow - Wizard of Oz).

Some of those science guys say we only use 10% of our brains. The idea that people manage to function normally while only using a miniscule part of the brain is complete and utter nonsense! BOOM! Take that science guys! There is NO scientific basis for the 10% brain myth. According to "How Stuff Works", this may come as a surprise -- accustomed as you probably are to the idea that nine-tenths of your brain's 100 billion or so neurons are wasting away in Margaritaville. But today's brain researchers, who have much more sophisticated tools than the old electrode-zappers, have discovered that the human brain doesn't seem to have any dormant regions. Additionally, if a human being only needed 10 percent of his or her brain to function normally, we'd be invulnerable to brain diseases (not to mention head traumas short of decapitation).

Author's note: The best way to kill a Zombie, decapitation.

The brain yearns to learn, it wants to be fed, and it is a GLUTTON for resources. Train your brain, play brain games, and exercise the brain too! There doesn't seem to be any portion of the brain that a person can lose without experiencing some sort of loss of function. If 90% were nonfunctioning, you would be comatose! (or a Zombie). It is true that different parts of the brain do different things, and not all at the same time. But while not every single ounce of that three-pound hunk of goo inside your skull is necessarily working at any given moment, brain scans show that over a 24-hour period, pretty much the whole brain gets a workout, and most of the parts are continually active. Even when you're sleeping, regions such as the frontal cortex, which controls higher-level thinking and self-awareness, and the somatosensory areas, which help you to sense your surroundings, remain active (How Does Stuff Work).

So how do we "use" our brain and exercise it? Here are 5 simple ways to increase your intelligence according to www.pickthebrain.com and anyone can squeeze a bit more productivity out of the old gray matter.

1. Minimize Television Watching – This is a hard sell. People love vegetating in front of the television, myself included more often than I'd like. The problem is watching television doesn't use your mental capacity OR allow it to recharge. It's like having the energy sapped out of a muscle without the health benefits of exercise. Don't you feel drained after a couple hours of TV? Your eyes are sore and tired from being focused on the light box for so long. You don't even have the energy to read a book. When you feel like relaxing, try reading a book instead. If you're too tired, listen to some music. When you're with your friends or family, leave the tube off and have a conversation. All of these things use your mind more than television and allow you to relax.

Author's note: They're heeeerrreeee…

2. Exercise – I used to think that I'd learn more by not exercising and using the time to read a book instead. But I realized that time spent exercising always leads to greater learning because it improves productivity during the time afterwards. Using your body clears your head and creates a wave of energy. Afterwards, you feel invigorated and can concentrate more easily.

Author's note: See Chapter One Again.

3. Read Challenging Books – Many people like to read popular suspense fiction, but generally these books aren't mentally stimulating. If you want to improve your thinking and writing ability you should read books that make you focus. Reading a classic novel can change your view of the world and will make you think in more precise, elegant English. Don't be afraid to look up a word if you don't know it, and don't be afraid of dense passages. Take your time, re-read when necessary, and you'll soon grow accustomed to the author's style. Once you get used to reading challenging books, I think you'll find that you aren't tempted to go back to page-turners. The challenge of learning new ideas is far more exciting than any tacky suspense-thriller.

4. Early to Bed, Early to Rise – Nothing makes it harder to concentrate than sleep deprivation. You'll be most rejuvenated if you go to bed early and don't sleep more than 8 hours. If you stay up late and compensate by sleeping late, you'll wake up lethargic and have trouble focusing. In my experience the early morning hours are the most tranquil and productive. Waking up early gives you more productive hours and maximizes your mental acuity all day. If you have the opportunity, take 10-20 minute naps when you are hit with a wave of drowsiness. Anything longer will make you lethargic, but a short nap will refresh you.

5. Take Time to Reflect – Often our lives get so hectic that we become overwhelmed without even realizing it. It becomes difficult to concentrate because nagging thoughts keep interrupting. Spending some time alone in reflection gives you a chance organize your thoughts and prioritize your responsibilities. Afterwards, you'll have a better understanding of what's important and what isn't. The unimportant stuff won't bother you anymore and your mind will feel less encumbered. I'm not saying you need to sit on the floor cross-legged and chant 'ohmmm'. Anything that allows a bit of prolonged solitude will do. One of my personal favorites is taking a solitary walk. Someone famous said, "All the best ideas occur while walking." I think he was on to something. Experiment to find the activity that works best for you.

I hope you aren't disappointed that none of the techniques I've proposed are revolutionary. But simple, unexciting answers are often the most valid. The challenge is having the will to adhere to them. If you succeed in following these 5 tips, you'll be rewarded with increased mental acuity and retention of knowledge.

So brain up! Using that brain for more than Zombie kibble will keep you from actually being Zombie kibble!

Chapter Twenty Five: Ask Questions Later...

A friend of mine once told me, "Shoot first and ask questions later." I was going to ask him "Why?" But I had already shot and killed him. While that story isn't true, you get the idea. This chapter will also go hand in hand with the next Chapter (26) on "Reaction Time" and Chapter 31 "Looking over your shoulder". What do these 3 chapters have in common? Watching your back and reacting accordingly, FAST!

We have often heard it said the "He who hesitates is lost." After the apocalypse it could be changed to "He who hesitates is DEAD!" If being confronted by a threat causes you to not take action or hesitate, you could be on the losing side of a fight, or dead. This doesn't mean that you should "whack" everyone you see, it does however mean that you need to be leery of everyone and be ready and able to react accordingly as fast as possible.

So how exactly do we do this? The best mentality is to be ready at all times for confrontation, even in non-hostile situations. Always have your firearm at the ready and don't have the "pacifist" attitude. The "I could never kill another human being" makes YOU a dead human being. If something feels "not right" trust your gut! Questioning yourself or the threat can be deadly. I would rather wonder if I eliminated threat or friend, than be dead.

Chapter Twenty Six: Reaction Time

A lot of the Chapters can cross reference to other Chapters. This one for instance can also tie in with Chapters 25 Asking Questions Later, 24 Using Your Brain, 18 Preparation Mentally, 10 Deadly Blows, and 1 Exercise. Why? Because reaction time is affected by all of these, OR they can be affected by your reaction time!

Let's lay it on the line, asking questions first (chapter 25) just took reaction out of the equation. If you exercise your brain (chapter 24) your reaction time quickens. When you are mentally prepared (chapter 18) your reaction to a situation is expected and second nature. A slow reaction can make your deadly blows (chapter 10) worthless. Working out your body, works out your mind (chapter 1 & 24) and essentially makes your reaction time faster.

So why is it important to have a fast reaction time? Ever watch an old western movie? The hero and the villain are in the middle of town, on a dusty street, and they are staring each other down. Sagebrush blows by, the town seems disserted, but we know the town folk have run and are hiding the buildings, peeking out the windows. Mothers are covering children's eyes, the villains' hand twitches to draw, and BANG! The town Hero stands behind a cloud of gun smoke, victorious, and alive. The reason? His reaction time is faster! Now… did his reaction time come natural? Was it genetic from his Mommy and Daddy? NO! The Hero practiced! He who practices A LOT will be faster. Bad guy or Good guy, doesn't matter after our apocalyptic disaster, there will be 2 left, the Quick and the Dead!

So practice reaction time, exercise your brain, exercise your fighting skills, be fast as lightning, and don't hesitate.

Chapter Twenty Seven: Natural (and Not So) Medicine

Nature has created MANY great natural medicines for us, and unless you are chemist, eventually your Aspirin is gonna go away. There are literally thousands of books on Natural Medicine, and having one in your possession is a great idea. I will cover some basics and some of my preferences, but again, this is by no means a complete list.

The absolute, most important, I cannot stress this enough, vital, advice in this chapter is… IDENTIFY THE PLANT FIRST! That being said, wild edible plants and medicinal plants are found everywhere in nature; but you have to make sure you can identify them. Many edible and medicinal plants have deadly poisonous look-alikes. A good field guide is invaluable.

Medicinal plants (agree or not) may be the only medicine we have in the future. Whether you like what is on this list or not, your mind may change if it's the only thing there is. This list of the 18 of Nature's Most Powerful Medicinal Plants comes from "WebEcoist - Going Beyond Green."

From marijuana to catnip, there are hundreds of remarkably common herbs, flowers, berries and plants that serve all kinds of important medicinal and health purposes that might surprise you: anti-inflammatory, anti-fungal, insect repellent, antiseptic, expectorant, antibacterial, detoxification, fever reduction, antihistamine

and pain relief. Here are eighteen potent medical plants you're likely to find in the

wild – or even someone's backyard – that can help with minor injuries, scrapes,

bites and pains.

Marijuana: Seriously. Though marijuana is still illegal in the most of the

United States, it is legal in 12 states for medicinal purposes, and if a case of poison

ivy in the woods isn't a medicinal purpose, what is? Marijuana was *mostly* legal

until 1970 when it became classified as a hard drug. No one thought of it as a

dangerous or illicit drug until the 20th century; in fact, hemp was George

Washington's primary crop and Thomas Jefferson's secondary crop. The

Declaration of Independence is written on it; the Gutenberg Bible was printed on

hemp, too. There's actually an environmental dimension to legalizing marijuana –

hemp is a remarkable and renewable plant, offering all kinds of foodstuff and

product uses that surpass cotton and plastic. But health benefits are well

documented, from depression and anxiety relief to reduced blood pressure, pain

alleviation and glaucoma treatment. It is not addictive, does not kill brain cells and

is not a "gateway" drug – in fact, when pot is more available, studies show that the

use of hard drugs like heroin and cocaine actually decreases. The bottom line for

hikers: when your leg is broken from a misjudged boulder hopping attempt (pain) and a bear has eaten your friend (depression) and you're lost because you forgot the compass (dumbass), consult the cannabis.

Author's note: These guys seem semi-sarcastic... I like them! Although I am not pro-marijuana, after an apocalypse, the mind may change.

Lady Ferns: If you grew up in the Pacific Northwest you likely know what ferns are good for: treating stinging nettles. One of the world's oldest plants, there are many varieties of ferns, but if you're lucky enough to spy the soft, delicate lady fern, grab some and roll it up between your palms into a rough mash. The juices released will quickly ease stinging nettle burns and can also ease minor cuts, stings and burns (fresh salt water also works in a pinch for bee stings). Bracken fern are similar to lady fern and will work, as well. The rougher, glossier, stiff sword fern and deer fern won't be as effective, though. (Learn about types of ferns.) Lady ferns actually grow all over North America but are common in areas with high rainfall.

California Poppy: The brilliant blooms of the poppy make this opioid plant an iconic one. The plant is an effective nervine (anxiety reliever) and is safe for use on agitated children. It can be made into a tea for quick relief of nervousness and tension. A stronger decoction will offer pain relief. (A decoction is made by "stewing" all safe plant parts, including stems and roots if possible, in water for several hours and, ideally, soaking overnight.)

Blood Flower: The blood flower (also Mexican butterfly weed) is a type of tropical milkweed with toxic milky sap that is emetic (it makes you hurl). It's also historically favored as a heart stimulant and worm expellant. Pretty useful for a number of potential hiking disasters, if you think about it. (Of course, if you'd quit eating those poisonous berries you probably wouldn't need to worry about finding a natural expectorant.)

Tansy: If you've decided to backpack through Europe instead of the mountains of Mexico (but why?), you'll want to know about a few helpful medicinal plants. Tansy is an old-world aster and remedy, used for flavoring beer and stews as well as repelling insects. Rubbing the leaves on the skin provides an effective bug repellent, but tansy can also be used to treat worms. It is said to be poisonous when extracted, but a few leaves are not harmful if ingested.

Korean Mint (hyssop): Who doesn't want to be minty fresh? Most of the various types of "mint" or mentha – spearmint, Korean mint, applemint, regular old mint – offer reported health benefits and medicinal properties. (Avoid pennyroyal, as it's poisonous.) Mint is famous for soothing headaches, fighting nausea, calming the stomach and reducing nervousness and fatigue. Korean mint, also called Indian mint and hyssop, is a fairly effective antiviral, making it useful for fighting colds and the flu. Whatever continent you're on, some type of mint is usually to be found. Eat whole, garnish food or make tea to get the all purpose health benefits.

Alfalfa: Alfalfa is fodder for livestock for a reason: it's incredibly rich in minerals and health-promoting nutrients and compounds. With roots that grow 20 to 30 feet deep, alfalfa is considered the "father of all plants". (It also contains a high amount of protein for a green.) Alfalfa originally grew in the Mediterranean and Middle East but has now spread to most of Europe and the Americans. It can treat morning sickness, nausea, kidney stones, kidney pain and urinary discomfort. It is a powerful diuretic and has a bit of stimulant power, helping to energize after a bout with illness. It's a liver and bowel cleanser and long-term can help reduce cholesterol. You can purchase seeds and sprouts, but it's fine to eat the leaves straight from the earth.

Catnip: The cannabis of the cat kingdom. Famous for making cats deliriously crazy, catnip has health properties that are great for humans, too. Catnip can relieve cold symptoms (helpful if you're on a camping trip and don't have access to Nyquil). It's useful in breaking a fever as it promotes sweating. Catnip also helps stop excessive bleeding and swelling when applied rather than ingested.

This mint plant (yep, another one) is also reportedly helpful in treating gas, stomach aches, and migraines. Catnip can stimulate uterine contractions, so it should not be consumed by pregnant women. It grows in the Northern Hemisphere.

Sage: Sage is an incredibly useful herb, widely considered to be perhaps the most valuable herb. It is anti-flammatory, anti-oxidant, and antifungal. In fact, according to the noted resource World's Healthiest Foods, "Its reputation as a panacea is even represented in its scientific name, Salvia officinalis, derived from the Latin word, salvere, which means 'to be saved'." It was used as a preservative for meat before the advent of refrigeration (eminently useful: you never know when you'll be forced to hunt in the wild). Sage aids digestion, relieves cramps, reduces diarrhea, dries up phlegm, fights colds, reduces inflammation and swelling, acts as a salve for cuts and burns, and kills bacteria. Sage apparently even brings color back to gray hair. A definite concern when lost in the woods.

Blackberries: Did you know blackberries have useful healing properties? Of course they're loaded in antioxidants and vitamins, but the leaves and roots have value, too. Native Americans have long used the stems and leaves for healing, while enjoying the young shoots peeled as a vegetable of sorts and the berries, either raw or in jams. The leaves and root can be used as an effective treatment against dysentery and diarrhea as well as serving usefulness as an anti-inflammatory and astringent. Ideal for treating cuts and inflammation in the mouth.

Wild Quinine: According to Alternative Nature Online, wild quinine is a potent herb that "is used as an antiperiodic, emmenagogue, kidney, lithontripic, poultice. It has traditionally been used in alternative medicine to treat debility, fatigue, respiratory infection, gastrointestinal infection, and venereal disease." Whatever the ailment, quinine is famously helpful in treating it. Only the root and flowers are edible; avoid the plant.

Navajo Tea: Also called greenthread, Plains Tea or Coyote Plant, this plant has been used for centuries by Native Americans to quickly relieve that most brutal and irritating of infections: the UTI (urinary tract infection). Best when made into a tea or decoction.

Red Clover: Native to Europe, Northern Africa and Western Asia, red clover is now ubiquitous worldwide. The plant's reddish pink blossoms can be used for coughs and colds, but they are an excellent detoxifier and blood cleanser as well.

Sweet Marjoram: Marjoram and oregano are often used interchangeably, but the aromatic sweet marjoram is slightly different. The Greeks called it the "Joy of the Mountain" and it was revered throughout the Mediterranean for its fragrance,

flavor and medicinal value. The famous French herbs de provence and Middle

Eastern za'atar both use sweet marjoram. Marjoram has many uses (it's a famous

digestive aid) but it is effective as an antifungal, antibacterial and disinfectant

treatment in a pinch.

Burdock Herb: Burdock, or cocklebur, is a prickly, thistle-like plant that

grows commonly in many parts of the world. It can get fairly big and its leaves

resemble the elephant ear plant. Though the burs often get caught in pets' and

livestock's fur, don't think of it only as an annoying plant. It is a highly effective

treatment against poison ivy and poison oak (claims that it cures cancer are slightly

less substantiated).

Feverfew: Feverfew is a plant that has well-known and documented health

properties and medicinal benefits. This anti-inflammatory can treat rheumatism,

arthritis and, most famously, migraine headaches and tension headaches. It's also

good for alleviating tension and general anxiety (it is a natural serotonin inhibitor).

It also helps to reduce swelling and bruising. Though feverfew is most effective

when taken daily, it can be a helpful pain reliever when no Advil is on hand.

Sweet Violet: Native to Europe and Asia, sweet violet is cultivated around the world and is a pleasant, delicate purple color. When brewed into a syrup the plant is effective as a treatment for colds, flu and coughs or sore throat. However, when made as a tea, it is wonderfully effective for relieving headaches and muscle and body pain.

Winter Savory: Winter savory is your savior against insect bites and stings. One of the most effective natural plant treatments for bug bites is originally from Europe and the Mediterranean but often shows up elsewhere thanks to global trade. In addition to being an antiseptic, it is delicious – used for flavoring meats and stews – and all parts are edible.

Author's note: In addition to plants, I would also like to offer up Essential Oils. I used to be a non-believer in the power of the oil, but after my wife got some of them and I used them, I am now a believer in the power of the oils! Essential Oils, what are they? My wife found a company called "doTerra" and she gets the oils from this company. I took this information straight from their website. If you are interested in Essential Oils, contact me and I will get you in contact with my wife. montanalee@usa.com

Essential oils are natural aromatic compounds found in the seeds, bark, stems, roots, flowers, and other parts of plants. They can be both beautifully and powerfully fragrant. If you have ever enjoyed the gift of a rose, a walk by a field of lavender, or the smell of fresh cut mint, you have experienced the aromatic qualities of essential oils. In addition to giving plants their distinctive smells, essential oils provide plants with protection against predators and disease and play a role in plant pollination.

Essential oils are non water-based phytochemicals made up of volatile aromatic compounds. Although they are fat soluble, they do not include fatty lipids or acids found in vegetable and animal oils. Essential oils are very clean, almost crisp, to the touch and are immediately absorbed by the skin. Pure, unadulterated essential oils are translucent and range in color from crystal clear to deep blue.

Try this at home: Squeeze the peel of a ripe orange. The fragrant residue on your hand is full of essential oils.

In addition to their intrinsic benefits to plants and being beautifully fragrant to people, essential oils have been used throughout history in many cultures for their medicinal and therapeutic benefits. Modern scientific study and trends toward more holistic approaches to wellness are driving a revival and new discovery of essential oil health applications.

dōTERRA CPTG Certified Pure Therapeutic Grade® essential oils represent the safest, purest, and most beneficial essential oils available today. They are gently and skillfully distilled from plants that have been patiently harvested at the perfect moment by experienced growers from around the world for ideal extract composition and efficacy. Experienced essential oil users will immediately recognize the superior quality standard for naturally safe, purely effective therapeutic-grade dōTERRA essential oils.

So now that we have discussed the medicine, let's talk edible plants. Direct from wildernesscollege.com is the following "Major Groupings of Wild Edible Plants".

There are so many different kinds of plants out there in the world. It can really help to initially lump them into more manageable groups. Here are some of the major groups of wild edibles, organized by plant families:

The Lily Family (Liliaceae): This includes species such as: Wild onions, Wild garlic, Wild leeks, Camas, and Glacier lilies.

The Purslane Family (Portulacaceae): This includes: Miner's Lettuce, Spring Beauty

The Rose Family (Rosaceae): This includes edible plants such as: Blackberry, Raspberry, Salmonberry, Thimbleberry, Wild roses, Hawthorn, Serviceberry, Choke-cherry, Wild strawberry, and Silverweed.

The Heath Family (Ericaceae): This includes species such as: Cranberry, Blueberry, and Huckleberry.

The Mustard Family (Brassicaceae): This includes plants such as: Pennycress, Shepard's purse, and Watercress.

The Mint Family (Lamiaceae): This includes wild edibles such as: Wild mint and Self-heal.

The Sunflower Family (Asteraceae): This includes species such as: Dandelion, Wild sunflower, Salsify, Chicory, Pineapple weed, Oxeye daisy, Common burdock, and Thistle species.

The Nettle Family (Urticaceae): This includes: Stinging nettle.

The Cattail Family (Typhaceae): This includes: Narrow-leaf and broad-leaved cattail.

The Beech Family (Fagaceae): This includes: Oaks, Chestnuts, and Beeches.

The Pine Family (Pinaceae): This includes trees such as: Pine, Hemlock, Douglas-fir, and Spruce.

Nature is amazing isn't she? I was surprised at some of things mentioned in this chapter myself, and this is just scratching the surface! Do some research and find out what plants in your area are medicine and/or food BEFORE you need them. If you are in a stressful situation, you may not be thinking clear and make a deadly mistake. I also suggest getting these plants and herbs now, dehydrating them, and stashing them now, while you can.

Chapter Twenty Eight: Never Underestimate Paracord

I LOVE paracord! I have knife lanyards made of paracord, bracelets, necklaces, key chains, a bike whip, belt, rifle sling, and more. LOVE LOVE LOVE! I am sure I have only touched the surface of the uses for paracord, and how to store it. Rather than put it in my backpack, I wear it.

Here are some great uses for paracord I have found from survivorgeek.com but let your imagination run wild! Also check out survivallife.com

#1 First of all, one of the main questions we get is, "How do you hold up your pants after you've taken apart your paracord Belt?" Well, after you take it apart, you should have 70 to 100 feet of paracord with which to form a makeshift belt or suspenders. (It's best to use a simple knot like a square knot that can easily be undone when you need to pull down your pants. Suspenders are easier, because you just slide them off your shoulders to take off your pants.)

#2 Repair torn clothing with the internal strands which slide easily out of the kernmantle (casing). Use a makeshift needle or be sure to keep one in your first-aid kit.

#3 Repair torn or broken equipment either by sewing or tying the pieces together securely

#4 Rig a makeshift tow rope. A single length of paracord has been tested to handle 550 lbs of weight, so wrap it securely 10 times and you have the ability to pull 5500 lbs.

#5 Securely tie down items to the top of a vehicle, or to protect them from a wind-storm

#6 String up a clothes line. Wet clothes are uncomfortable when you're camping and dangerous when you're trying to survive.

#7 Hang a bear bag to keep your food away from critters. This is good whether you're camping or roughing it in the woods

#8 Replace your shoe laces. Just burn the ends and thread them through.

#9 Replace a broken Zipper pull

#10 Use it as dental floss. Pull out the internal strands and keep up your hygiene even in the woods, or to get that pesky piece of meat out from between your teeth.

#11 Tie things to your backpack with it so you can carry more stuff hands free

#12 Secure an animal to a tree or post, or make a leash

#13 Tie up a person (heh heh heh)

#14 String up a trip wire to protect an area…rig it with bells, or cans or make a fancier trap

#15 Lower yourself or an object very carefully down from a height. (note: paracord is NOT climbing rope, and is NOT a realistic replacement for true climbing rope; do not expect it to catch you should you fall. For security double or triple the thickness if you can)

#16 Rig a pulley system to lift a heavy object

#17 Make a ladder to get up or down

#18 Tie up a tarp or poncho to make an awning to keep off sun or rain

#19 If you're hiking in a place where there is danger of avalanche tie yourself to your buddy so you can find each other should one of you get caught under snow

#20 Keep your stuff. Tie objects you're likely to drop around your wrist, ankle, or waist

#21 Make a pack by first making a netting then adding a draw-string

Roughing it in the outdoors…Many of the uses above could be handy in the woods, but here are some options specific to outdoor survival:

#22 Build a shelter using sticks or by tying up the corners of a poncho or tarp

#23 Rig an improvised hammock (in case you haven't sprung for a real hammock)

#24 Make a snare out of the internal strands

#25 Lash logs or other items together to build a raft.

#26 Tie snow shoes. Bend a 1" branch in a teardrop shape. Tie it securely then weave the paracord back and forth across the opening. Tie this to your shoes.

#27 Use it to make a bow drill for fire starting...(note it does take a lot of practice to start a fire with a bow, so don't rely on this unless you've done it before!)

#28 Make a sling to throw stones for protection and food.

#29 Use it for signaling by tying a mirror or colorful cloth to the top of a tree

#30 Use it to make a bola for hunting large birds

Fishing applications:

#31 Make fishing line by cutting a length and pulling out the internal strands (there are seven of them, each of which comes apart into two, so there's 14 thin lines if you aren't catching really big fish). Just tie them together.

#32 Make a fish stringer. If you've just pulled the strings out to make fishing line, the remaining kernmantle (the colored sheath) would be plenty strong enough to hold fish. Otherwise just cut a length, and tie through the gills.

#33 Secure your boat or raft

#34 Make a net out of the internal strands…if you have some time on your hands

First aid uses:

#35 Tie straight sticks around a broken limb to make a splint.

#36 Tie a sling to hold your arm

#37 Sew up a wound using the internal strands. For thinner thread untwist one of the internal strands

#38 Make a tourniquet to slow loss of blood

#39 Make a stretcher by running paracord between two long sticks, or fashion a branch drag to move an injured person

What a great list! And this is just SOME of the great uses. I'm sure there are at least 100 out there, and maybe even more. I just recently removed a broken plastic handle off my machete and wrapped the tang in paracord. You are only limited by your imagination, and there are so many colors out there its mind boggling. Go have some fun!

My daughter Parker makes Paracord bracelets, key chains, and more!

Chapter Twenty Nine: Buddy System (or Why Fight It Alone)

I have already spoken of Groups and the importance of them. Many people however are loners. Not necessarily a "bad" thing, but there is a lot to be said about having a partner. Genesis 2:18 "And the Lord God said, "It is not good that the man should be alone; I will make him a helper fit for him." Things are always easier when someone "has your back." When we spoke of enclosed places looking for supplies, a guard outside while another searches, even having someone to carry on an intelligent conversation with is nice. Remember the movie "Castaway" with Tom Hanks? Dude went nuts talking to "Wilson" his "friend" that's a volleyball. Human interaction is a natural, with very few sane exceptions. Surviving any situation is easier when someone has your back. I have been in fights that, if I had been alone, could have been VERY bad. It was nice having a backup in those situations.

Being alone can cause: feelings of being inadequate, Lack of support, loneliness, being alone makes you a preferred target, social skills dwindle, and no one to be held accountable to.

While these may seem trivial, remember, there is strength in numbers.

Chapter Thirty: First Aid

This is an entire book all by itself and we all know it. If you don't know basic First-Aid, get a book, take a class, or an advanced class even. Until you can perform an emergency tracheotomy with a steak knife and a ball point pen, you need more lessons. I'm not going to teach you how to do First Aid. I am going to teach you where to find great First Aid items to use, both now and in the event of the apocalyptic event.

The absolute best thing to do is to stock up now! The local Dollar Store has simple first aid kits, band aids, ointments, etc. Buy a lot and buy cheap! If our apocalyptic event has already happened you may struggle to find supplies. Check the obvious places first; drug stores, grocery stores, convenience stores, etc. But there are some places you may not think to look for supplies. Here is my list of strange places First Aid supplies are hiding.

1. Corporate offices – most employers are required to have First Aid kits on the premises for employees.
2. Cars – check the glove compartment, trunk, truck box, or under the seat. May find other goodies too!
3. Large Trucks – I'm talking about the haulers and eighteen wheelers, they have their lives in those trucks and you will be surprised what you may find.

4. Fast Food Joints – the back room of Joe's Burgers is a great place to look. The food may be gone, but other supplies may still be hanging out. Maybe knives, cooking utensils, towels, aprons, and even our First Aid supplies.

5. Beauty supply stores and Salons – Scissors, razors, antibiotics, and more!

6. Clothing stores – again, the employees are careless, even if the clothes are all gone, there may be other nifty items. Some of those nice chrome displays may make a good BO staff or club.

7. Industrial locations – factories, mills, mechanics shops, manufacturers, or any other place that has manual labor. Remember, other cool things can be found here too!

Just because it doesn't say "Pharmacy" on the building, don't discount the things you may find. Be open to searching and be creative, see the potential in everything.

Chapter Thirty One: Looking Over Your Shoulder

Chapter 2 addresses this in a "double" mentality. Making sure by checking twice is twice as nice at half the price. In other words, look again. Remember when you were little and crossing the street for the first time and your Mommy said, "Look left, look right, and look left again." Go thank your Mom! She was right and looking to protect you. She is the reason you haven't been hit by a car crossing the street. If you HAVE been hit by a car when crossing the street, it's what you deserve for not listening to your Mom!

When hunting with my Dad, my sons, and my daughters, every time we have been stalking a deer, inevitably the deer has doubled back and ended up behind us. I know this, my kids know this, and my Dad taught me this! This is why none of us have ever been "skunked" when hunting. Keeping this in mind, take the mentality of the deer, now you are the hunted. Do you think that if the deer knew I was going to be checking behind me, the deer would have got behind me? No, I think not. The deer would have paralleled us while we walked.

Always check behind you for game and adversaries. It also gives you a different perspective on the terrain. When approaching a hill when driving, if you keep looking forward after you pass it, you will have no idea what was hiding there. But if you turn around, you may be surprised what you find! I have seen old cabins, old cars, animals, etc. All because my perspective changed and I double checked. It is also handy for not getting lost; if you remember what is behind you from looking back, you may be able to trigger that memory when retreating back that direction.

The most important reason to watch your back though, is so you don't get snuck up on. If you're not looking back, you could get stabbed in the back. It's simple really, every so often turn around and assess the surroundings. If could make the difference in survival.

Chapter Thirty Two: The Finer Things In Life

Scotch and a cigar again come to mind again! But that's not what this chapter is about. This chapter is actually about being frugal and cheap. If you're a brand name wearing type, get over it! "I only wear X brand jeans." That's going to work out great for you after an apocalyptic event and all the children in foreign countries aren't at the factory making your brand of jeans anymore.

You get what you get and don't throw a fit. My kids know this one well. We are a thrifty house, we use coupons a LOT, and 'Generic" is a brand name in our home! The TV can tell you all day long that X is better than Z, and I ask them why? It's not really, read the ingredients, they are identical. The reason one is more expensive is because they spend more on advertising. 70% of the cost of most items is advertising. So a less expensive item you have never heard of, obviously doesn't waste money on advertising.

The point is, that when you are wandering from place to place, don't look a gift horse in the mouth! Tuna is tuna, a towel is a towel, and a tampon is a tampon. If you're hungry, you'll eat it! If you're wet you'll use it! If you're... nevermind...

Chapter Thirty Three: Tools

Tools are valuable for building, fixing, and killing. Yes… killing. A chainsaw is great for cutting wood for building and for fires, but did you know it can remove a head and other limbs? It CAN! There are many tools that can double as "other" items also and here is my list:

1. Hammer – used for pounding nails, and pounding skulls.

2. Screwdriver - used for putting in screws, and as a knife or ice pick.

3. Ice pick – used for chipping ice, and as a shank

4. Ice scraper – used for scraping ice, decapitator, and spear.

5. Pipe wrench – Great for pipework, and for smashing bones, skulls, etc.

6. Pliers – Used for pinching, tightening, and for torture and pulling teeth, etc.

7. Hoe – Great for gardening, and for decapitation.

8. Rake – Raking, and skewering.

9. Shovel – Shoveling, and slicing, decapitating, breaking bone, etc.

10. Nails and Screws – For building, also as shrapnel in IED's (Improvised Explosive Device).

11. Tin Snips – Good for cutting thin metal, and cutting fingers off and tongues out of interrogated people.

12. Box Cutter – for slicing and trimming, and for slicing and killing.

13. Tire Iron – For changing tires on a vehicle, and for smashing skulls

14. Spud Bar – Good for helping in digging holes, also a good smasher of bone.

By no means is this a complete list, but take away electricity and gas and we are limited to the hand tools. Use your imagination when you carry tools with you, as to what else they can be used for.

Chapter Thirty Four: A Little Faith

The LORD is my shepherd; I shall not want. He maketh me to lie down in green pastures: he leadeth me beside the still waters. He restoreth my soul: he leadeth me in the paths of righteousness for his name's sake. Yea, though I walk through the valley of the shadow of death, I will fear no evil: for thou art with me; thy rod and thy staff they comfort me. Thou preparest a table before me in the presence of mine enemies: thou anointest my head with oil; my cup runneth over. Surely goodness and mercy shall follow me all the days of my life: and I will dwell in the house of the LORD forever. Psalm 23.

A little faith can go a long way, and if you have no faith, what do you have to live for? Faith in the human race surviving, faith in surviving yourself, faith of the group surviving, faith in a higher power, faith in those around you, faith in your group, faith in civilization, faith in abilities, faith in love, faith in the Bible, faith in a better world, faith in family, faith in my tools, and faith in my weapons.

Without faith, none of these are any good. I believe they will work, so I use them assuming they actually will.

In the introduction I discussed what some believe, going away before the apocalypse (rapture), after it happens, during the event, and regardless of what you believe, you have to have faith in something. Even if it's simple faith that someday it will all be over, the pain, the suffering, the struggling, the insecurity, the death, and the hurt. Have faith in something; otherwise you will have no desire to go on.

If you have no faith in Jesus, and you want to, please contact a local Pastor at a local Bible Believing Christian Church.

Get support, fellowship, and the communion of a group. A group called followers of Christ, Christians. That's how you become the ultimate survivor. leethalbiker@gmail.com – Leethal

In Conclusion...

First, thanks for taking this warped little journey of sarcasm, profitable zombie hunting, and Faith with me. I hope you learned something, laughed, or maybe had a life changing moment. I had fun, laughed a lot, and learned some fun stuff too. While some pages might be morbid or "less than pleasant", I hope overall you were shaking your head with a smile on your face, trying to imagine what a crazy type of person I am.

While the eradication of Zombies may not be a realistic way to make a living (yet), certain sociological tidbits contained in the book may offer insight to the future of our economic status. Our world seems to be collapsing around us more each day, and while Zombies may be a metaphor for our impending doom, it really pays to be prepared for a worst case scenario. I tell my friends, "I'm not paranoid. I prepare for the worst, and pray for the best."

I truly hope this generation never has to see the worst of mankind, economical disaster, or social destruction. It does seem inevitable though, that it may happen. Maybe not to the worst imaginable level, but I see an increase each day to the destruction of mankind. I suppose if we have to go through it, we might as well all have a little fun! Feed your brain, laugh a lot, and have some faith. Read all you can and make your own decisions about the world around you and don't let anyone tell you what to believe. Laugh about everything! Life is short and no one gets out alive. I've been told the odds are one out of every one person dies and those are pretty good odds! So find opportunities to laugh daily. Faith is a pivotal part of existence, if you don't have faith in something; there is nothing to strive on for. Have faith in something. If you can't have faith in the government, faith in mankind, or faith in things, maybe try faith in God.

If I offended you, sorry, it's all in fun, and really, there is some useful info in this book. Remember to "Keep Calm, and Zombie On!" Hope you have a great Apocalypse/Rapture, and God Bless.

If you would like to order a copy of my other book, please go to: www.lulu.com/leethal There you will find "Apocalypse Survival (Zombie or Otherwise)"

If you would like to also have a degree in Zombilogy, contact me at leethalbiker@gmail.com It's a simple 10 question test based on Zombie movies, Zombie TV Shows, and my books for $5.00 to get an Associate degree, 20 question test and $10 for a Bachelor degree, 30 question test and $20 for a Masters degree, and if you want the Doctorate in Zombilogy it's a whopping 50 question test and $25.00. Remember, this is a souvenir diploma from a phony college, which is nothing more than a nice certificate to hang on your wall as a conversation piece. It's for fun; you're not going to get a job with it... really... it just proves you have Zombie knowledge. As stated above, you get the test, and upon successfully completing the test (70% or better) I will mail you out a nice "Diploma" to display on your wall. Suitable for framing, swatting flies, or starting fires.

About the Author:

Leethal (Lee Williams) was born in Billings, MT in 1967. Leethal is the son

of an Electrician, Grandson of a Rancher, and a Grandson of a Southern Baptist

Music Minister, all godly Men. Leethal was the last of a generation whose Mother

stayed home to take care of the house and kids. A task he has been convicted of

with his own family. Which financially is almost impossible in today's world. A

disabled Navy Veteran, a former 12-year Radio DJ, and Circulation Manager for

the local newspaper; Graduated from Colstrip High School in 1985, Associate

degree in Journalism and Broadcasting in 1990, a Bachelor of Science in Human

Services & Business management 2012 (with Honors), and a Doctorate in

Zombilogy 2014. (This is not a real degree. Laugh with me here people!) Leethal is

a biker and rides a Harley! He is married to his soul mate Kelly and has one

adopted son & one blood son from a previous marriage, two bonus daughters from

his wife Kelly, and three grandchildren. He and his family live in Belgrade and

attend bike rallies and events whenever and where ever possible.

References & Credits

The Holy Bible

Zombieland the movie

http://www.livestrong.com

http://www.mycheme.com

http://www.isu.edu/outdoor/survkit.htm

http://www.andrewjackwriting.com/2012/01/25/10-hand-to-hand-combat-myths-that-

writers-need-to-stop-using/

http://www.wikihow.com/Be-Good-at-Hand-to-Hand-Combat

http://www.wikihow.com/Disable-an-Adversary-in-Hand-to-Hand-Combat

http://adventure.howstuffworks.com/survival/wilderness/live-without-food-and-

water1.htm

http://www.military.com/special-operations/seal-training-mental-preparation.html

Wizard of Oz the movie

http://www.pickthebrain.com/blog/5-simple-ways-to-make-the-most-of-your-

intelligence/

http://www.wildernesscollege.com/wild-edible-plants.html

http://www.survivorgeek.com/pages/Emergency-uses-for-Paracord.html

http://www.survivallife.com